## MULTICULTURAL SEASONAL CRAFTS

# SPRING CRAFTS FROM DIFFERENT CULTURES

## 12 Projects to Celebrate the Season

### BY MEGAN BORGERT-SPANIOL

a Capstone company — publishers for children

Raintree is an imprint of Capstone Global Library Limited, a company incorporated in England and Wales having its registered office at 264 Banbury Road, Oxford, OX2 7DY – Registered company number: 6695582

**www.raintree.co.uk**
myorders@raintree.co.uk

Hardback edition © Capstone Global Library Limited 2023
Paperback edition © Capstone Global Library Limited 2024

The moral rights of the proprietor have been asserted. All rights reserved. No part of this publication may be reproduced in any form or by any means (including photocopying or storing it in any medium by electronic means and whether or not transiently or incidentally to some other use of this publication) without the written permission of the copyright owner, except in accordance with the provisions of the Copyright, Designs and Patents Act 1988 or under the terms of a licence issued by the Copyright Licensing Agency, 5th Floor, Shackleton House, 4 Battle Bridge Lane, London, SE1 2HX (www.cla.co.uk). Applications for the copyright owner's written permission should be addressed to the publisher.

**British Library Cataloguing in Publication Data**
A full catalogue record for this book is available from the British Library.

ISBN 978 1 3982 4533 4 (hardback)
ISBN 978 1 3982 4534 1 (paperback)

**Editorial Credits**
Editor: Jessica Rusick
Designer: Sarah DeYoung
Originated by Capstone Global Library Ltd

**Image Credits**
Mighty Media, Inc.: projects and materials; Shutterstock: Bernardo Emanuelle, 26 (photograph), Jaimie D. Travis, 5 (hole punch), Peter Kotoff, 16 (tablet)

Design Elements
Shutterstock: KALYA MALYA, lukeruk, sherilhome

All the internet addresses (URLs) given in this book were valid at the time of going to press. However, due to the dynamic nature of the internet, some addresses may have changed, or sites may have changed or ceased to exist since publication. While the author and publisher regret any inconvenience this may cause readers, no responsibility for any such changes can be accepted by either the author or the publisher.

## CONTENTS

Spring .................................... 4

Holi ...................................... 6

St Patrick's Day .......................... 8

Passover ................................. 10

Easter ................................... 12

Hanami ................................... 14

April Fools' Day ......................... 16

Songkran ................................. 18

Earth Day ................................ 20

Ramadan .................................. 22

Wesak .................................... 24

Mother's Day ............................. 26

Cinco de Mayo ............................ 28

   Find out more ....................... 32

   About the author .................... 32

# Spring

What is your favourite part of spring? Is it the blossoming flowers or baby animals? Maybe it's all the seasonal celebrations, including Holi, Earth Day and Cinco de Mayo!

Celebrate spring with cool projects that reflect the season. Craft your own Easter bottle planters or Ramadan lanterns. You might even make sponge soakers for the Thai New Year or fake spilt milk for April Fools' Day. Spring is filled with enough natural beauty and festivities to keep you crafting all season long!

# BASIC SUPPLIES

 craft foam

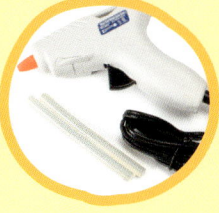 hot glue gun

 felt pens

 paint and paintbrushes

 hole punch

 pencil

 ruler

 tissue paper

 string

white glue

# CRAFTING TIPS

**Be prepared!** Read through the materials and instructions before starting a project. Cover your workspace with paper or plastic to protect it from messes or spills.

**Think outside the book!** Lots of the projects in this book use materials you'll probably find around your home. Is there something you can't find? Think of ways to adapt the project using items you do have.

**Ask first!** Get permission before using materials you find at home or school. Also ask before you collect items from nature and bring them indoors.

**Be safe!** Ask an adult for help with projects that require sharp or hot tools.

**Clean up!** When your project is complete, put all materials and tools back where you found them. Clean up any spills and wipe down your crafting surface.

## HOLI
# Colour burst wall hanging

Holi is a Hindu celebration widely known as the Festival of Colours. In its most famous tradition, people throw brightly coloured powder and scented water at each other. Holi marks the beginning of spring and the triumph of good over evil. Create a wall hanging inspired by this colourful holiday!

## What you need

- cardboard
- pencil
- scissors
- craft knife (optional)
- string
- ruler
- stapler
- wool
- hot glue gun

## What you do

1. Trace and cut a shape out of cardboard. Make it the size you want your wall hanging to be. If you are using thick cardboard, ask an adult to help you cut out the shape using a craft knife.

2. Cut a 30-centimetre (12-inch) piece of string. Staple the ends of the string to the back of the cardboard shape to make a hanger.

3. Cut another piece of cardboard that is 7.5 cm (3 in) wide and 10 cm (4 in) long.

4. Loosely wrap a length of wool around the width of the cardboard piece about 60 times.

5. Slide the wool loop off the cardboard. Use another piece of wool to tie a knot around the middle of the loop.

6. Cut open the loops on either side of the knot. This creates a pom-pom.

7. Trim the pom-pom so the wool is the same length all around.

8. Repeat steps 4 to 7 to make more pom-poms. Use different sizes of cardboard frames to create different sizes of pom-poms.

9. Arrange the pom-poms on your cardboard wall hanging. Once you like how they look, glue them down. Then hang up your pom-pom colour burst!

## ST. PATRICK'S DAY
# Pot of gold

The leprechaun is a well-known symbol of St Patrick's Day, a celebration of the patron saint of Ireland. These elf-like creatures from Irish folklore are mischievous protectors of their pots of gold treasure. Create a fun leprechaun's hat that doubles as a pot of gold!

## What you need

- small, clean terracotta pot
- green paint and paintbrush
- scissors
- black electrical tape
- yellow craft foam
- ruler
- craft knife
- hot glue gun
- gold-wrapped chocolates

## What you do

1. Paint a small, clean terracotta pot green. Let the paint dry.

2. Wrap black electrical tape around the pot just below the rim.

3. Cut a craft foam square that is 4 cm (1.5 in) on each side. This is the hat's buckle. Ask an adult to help you cut a small square out of the centre of the buckle using a craft knife.

4. Glue the buckle to the black tape.

5. Fill your leprechaun's hat with gold-wrapped chocolates to share!

## PASSOVER
# Painted rock frog

The Jewish festival of Passover remembers the story of the Israelites escaping enslavement in ancient Egypt. Frogs have a star role in this story. They were one of ten plagues sent upon Egypt by God to encourage the Pharaoh to free the enslaved people. Make your own Passover frog to accompany this story of freedom.

## What you need

- smooth stones
- paint (dark green, white, black, light green) and paintbrushes
- pencil
- cotton bud
- hot glue gun
- wooden dowel
- black felt pen

## What you do

1. Pick out stones to build your frog. Choose oval stones for the body and head; narrow oval stones for the legs and small, circular stones for the feet and eyes.

2. Paint the stones dark green. Let them dry.

3. Use a pencil eraser and cotton bud to add details to the eye stones with white and black paint.

4. Glue the head onto the body stone. Glue the eye stones on top of the head.

5. Glue the leg stones on either side of the body stone. Glue the feet stones to the base of the legs.

6. Add spots and other details to the frog's body using a wooden dowel dipped in light green paint.

7. Add nose and mouth details to the frog's head with a black felt pen. Then make a lily pad using a flat, circular stone painted light green.

## EASTER

# Baby chick bottle planters

Easter is a Christian holiday celebrating Jesus Christ and his return to life after death. For many, Easter also marks a time of rebirth in nature. That's why eggs, bunnies and chicks are common symbols of Easter. Grow some new plant life in a baby chick bottle to celebrate Easter!

## What you need

- empty, clear plastic bottle (size can vary)
- scissors or craft knife
- hole punch
- yellow paint and paintbrush
- orange and yellow craft foam
- hot glue gun
- permanent marker pen
- string
- ruler
- soil
- small plant

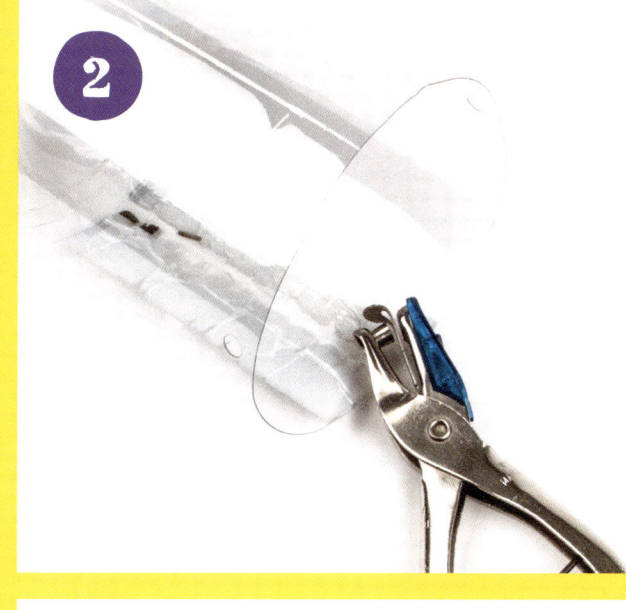

## What you do

1. Ask an adult to help you cut off the top third of the bottle.

2. Punch three holes around the cut edge of the bottle. The holes should be equally spaced from each other.

3. Paint the outside of the bottle yellow. Let the paint dry.

4. Cut a triangle out of orange craft foam for a beak. Glue the beak to the bottle. Cut two teardrop shapes out of yellow craft foam for the wings. Glue them to the bottle.

5. Add eyes to the bottle using permanent marker pen.

6. Cut three pieces of string 60 cm (24 in) long. Tie a knot at one end of each piece. The knots should be larger than the holes punched into the bottle.

7. Thread the string through the holes in the bottle so the knots are on the outside. Then knot the other ends of the string together at the top.

8. Have an adult help you fill the bottle with soil and a plant.

9. Hang your baby chick planter from a hook or tree branch!

## HANAMI
# Cherry blossom bundle

Hanami is a Japanese tradition of welcoming spring and enjoying its natural beauty. Festivities are planned around the annual blooming of cherry blossom trees. Use collected sticks and twigs to create a cheerful cherry blossom bundle for your coffee table!

### Fun fact

Hanami means "flower viewing" in Japanese. Families and friends gather for picnics beneath flowering cherry blossom trees to celebrate Hanami.

## What you need

- string
- ruler
- scissors
- sticks and twigs
- pink and white tissue paper
- thick marker pen
- hot glue gun
- buttons or beads

## What you do

1. Cut a piece of string 46 cm (18 in) long. Lay it horizontally across your work surface. Place a group of sticks and twigs vertically over the middle of the string.

2. Tie the string around the sticks to create a bundle. Knot the string and cut off any excess.

3. Cut out several squares of pink and white tissue paper. The squares should be 4 cm (1.5 in) on each side.

4. Wrap a tissue paper square around the base of a thick marker pen to form a flower petal shape. Glue the flower petal to a stick in the bundle.

5. Repeat step 4 to fill the bundle with flower petals.

6. Glue a button or bead to the centre of each flower petal. Then place the bundle on a coffee table for everyone to see!

## APRIL FOOLS' DAY
# Fake spilt milk

In many cultures, the first day of April is a time for pranks, tricks and jokes. Historians are not sure how this tradition began. Whatever its origins, April Fools' Day inspires hijinks around the world. Try fooling your friends and family with this fake spilt milk!

## What you need

- paper cup
- measuring spoon
- white glue
- white paint
- craft stick
- wax paper
- scissors

## What you do

1. In a paper cup, mix together 30 ml of white glue and 15 ml of white paint.

2. Cut a square of wax paper. Tip the cup sideways onto the wax paper so the glue mixture spills out.

3. Leave the cup lying sideways on the wax paper and let the glue dry. This will take about 48 hours.

4. Make sure the mixture is completely dry before carefully peeling it off the wax paper.

5. Place your fake spilt milk on the carpet, a computer keyboard or anywhere it will get attention!

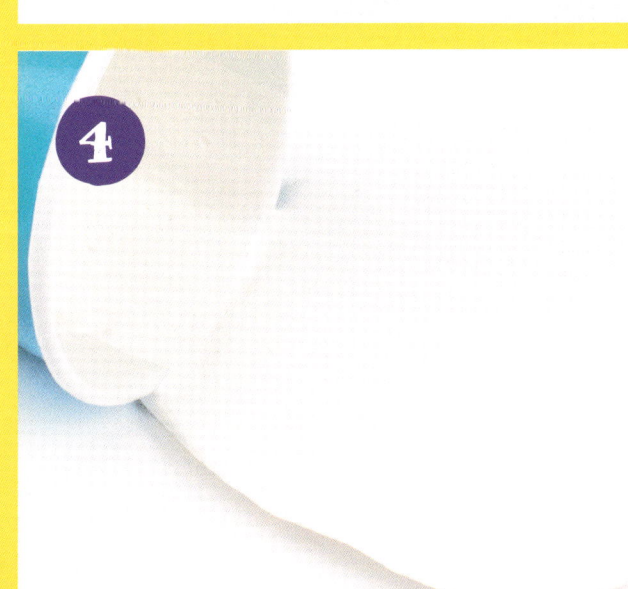

## Fun fact

On 1 April 1957, the BBC TV show Panorama reported a heavy spaghetti crop from trees in southern Switzerland. Some viewers knew the story was fake. Others wanted to know how they could grow their own spaghetti!

## SONGKRAN
# Sponge soakers

Songkran marks the Buddhist New Year. To celebrate, people hold joyful water fights in the streets of Thailand. The water symbolizes washing away bad luck of the previous year. Make your own Songkran water soakers out of sponges and string!

### Fun fact
Songkran is mainly associated with Thailand. But Laos, Cambodia and other Southeast Asian countries celebrate the new year with similar water festivals.

## What you need

- rectangular sponges
- scissors
- string
- ruler
- bucket of water

## What you do

1. Take three sponges. Cut each sponge along its length into three equal strips.

2. Cut a piece of string 45 cm (18 in) long. Lay it horizontally across your work surface.

3. Stack the nine sponge strips in three layers of three. If your sponges are different colours, use a mix of colours in each layer. Place the sponge stack vertically over the middle of the string.

4. Tie the string tightly around the middle of the sponge strips. Double-knot the string and cut off any excess length.

5. Repeat steps 1 to 4 to make more sponge soakers. Then dunk them in a bucket of water and start throwing them!

EARTH DAY

# Tinned herb garden

Earth Day was first observed in the United States in 1970. It marked the beginning of a national effort to reduce pollution and protect the environment. Since then, Earth Day has become a global event. Many people celebrate the day by planting trees. You can take part by planting an indoor herb garden!

## What you need

- empty tins
- hammer and nail
- white paint and paintbrush
- string
- ruler
- scissors
- hot glue gun
- black duct tape
- white paint pen
- potting soil
- herb plants, such as sage, mint, parsley and oregano
- tray or coaster
- water

## What you do

1. Rinse and dry a tin for each herb you want to plant.

2. Ask an adult to make three drainage holes in the bottom of each tin using a hammer and nail.

3. Paint the tins white. Let them dry.

4. Cut two 68-cm (27-in) lengths of string for each tin. Glue the string around the top and bottom of each tin.

5. Make labels for the plants by writing their names in white paint pen on pieces of black duct tape.

6. Have an adult help you fill each tin with soil and a herb plant.

7. Place your herb plants on a tray or coaster near a sunny window. Water them regularly and watch your garden grow!

# RAMADAN
# Lantern light catchers

Ramadan is the ninth month of the Islamic calendar. During this time of prayer and fasting, decorative lanterns light up the night. Try making your own Ramadan lanterns that catch sunlight during the day!

**Fun fact**

Traditional Ramadan lanterns are called fanous in Arabic.

## What you need

- pencil
- ruler
- black card
- scissors
- craft knife (optional)
- tissue paper
- glue stick
- hole punch
- string

## What you do

1. Use a pencil and ruler to draw the outline of a lantern on black card. An easy way to draw a lantern is to start with a rectangle and add a pointed dome to each of the shorter ends. Cut out the lantern.

2. Draw shapes to create windows on the lantern. Use scissors to cut out the windows. Or ask an adult to help you cut them out with a craft knife.

3. Cut pieces of tissue paper that are slightly bigger than the lantern's windows. Glue the tissue paper over the window openings.

4. Punch a hole in the top of the lantern. Thread a piece of string through the hole and knot it to make a hanger for your lantern.

5. Repeat steps 1 to 4 to create other lantern designs to fill your windows!

## WESAK
# Floating lotus flower

Wesak, also called Vesak, celebrates the birthday of Buddha, the founder of Buddhism. For Buddhists, the lotus flower symbolizes enlightenment and rebirth. Many Buddhist cultures include lotus flowers in their Wesak decorations and rituals. You can make your own lotus flower out of plastic spoons!

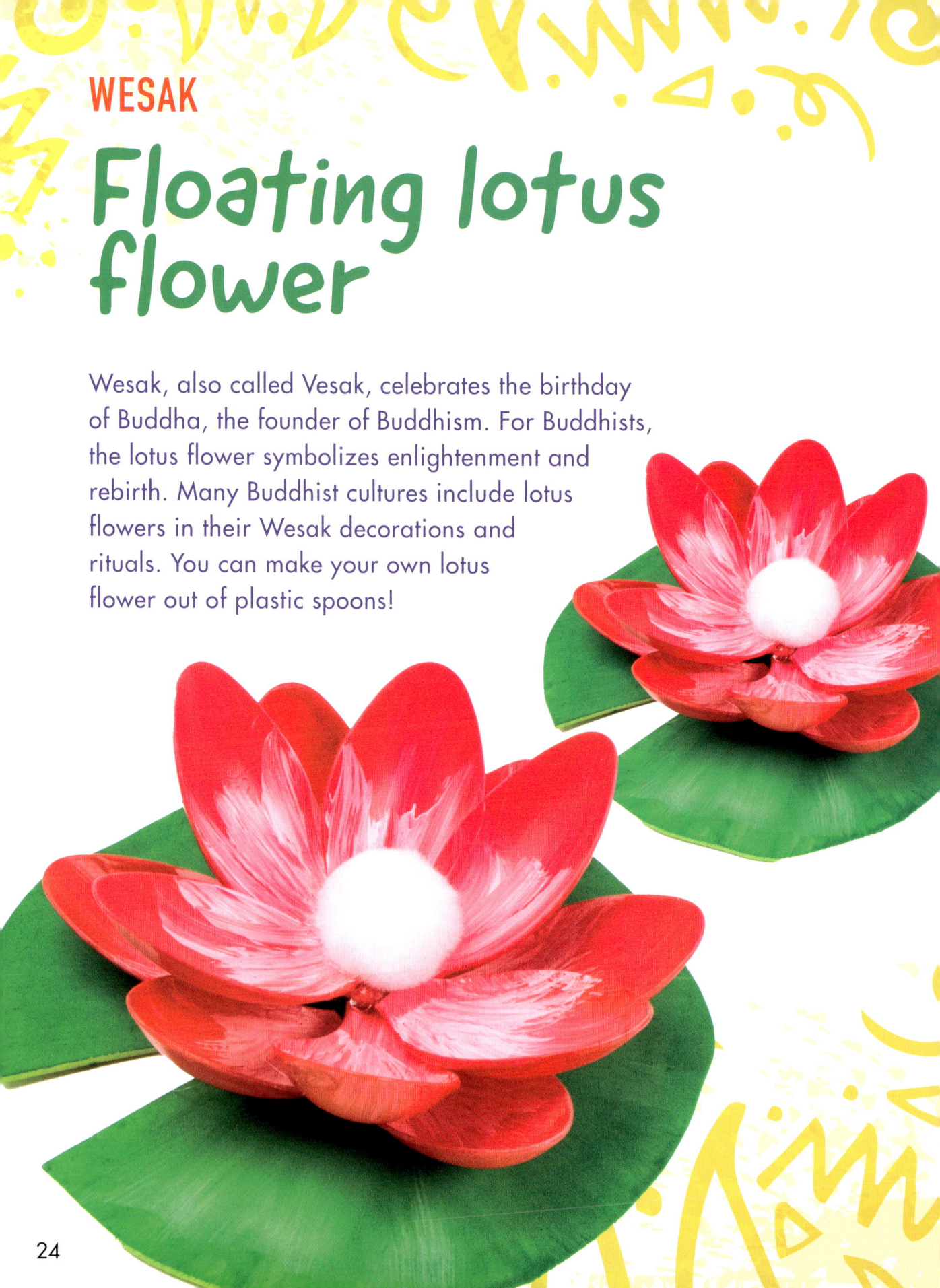

## What you need

- 12 plastic spoons
- pruning shears
- paint (any colour, plus white and green) and paintbrushes
- green craft foam
- scissors
- ruler
- hot glue gun
- pom-pom
- bowl of water

## What you do

1. Ask an adult to help you break the handles off the spoons using pruning shears or a similar tool.

2. Paint the spoon heads a color of your choice. Brush white paint up the middle of each spoon to create a gradient. Let the paint dry.

3. Cut a circular lily pad out of green craft foam. It should be about 13 cm (5 in) across. Use green and white paint to add dimension to the lily pad.

4. Glue three spoon heads to the lily pad so the cut ends point towards the middle.

5. Glue three more spoon heads in between the first three.

6. Glue the last six spoon heads to fill in the spaces between the first six. Glue a pom-pom in the centre of the spoon petals.

7. Place your lotus flower in a bowl of water and watch it float!

## MOTHER'S DAY
# Paper flower frame

Cultures around the world celebrate motherhood in different ways. In the UK, people celebrate Mother's Day by giving flowers and other gifts to a mother or female caregiver. Show appreciation for someone in your life with a framed photo of the two of you!

### Fun fact
Mother's Day has been celebrated in the UK since the 16th century. It falls on the fourth Sunday in Lent.

## What you need

- bowl 15 to 20 cm (6 to 8 in) across
- pen
- old magazines
- ruler
- marker pen
- scissors
- hot glue gun
- picture frame
- paint and paintbrush (optional)
- photo

## What you do

1. Trace the bowl on a sheet of thick magazine paper. Cut out the circle.

2. Starting along the edge of the circle, cut a spiral in towards the centre. The strip of paper you cut should be about 1.3 cm to 2.5 cm (½ inch to 1 inch) wide.

3. Begin rolling up the spiral from the outside end. Glue it every few centimetres until you've reached the centre. Then glue the centre of the spiral to the bottom of the roll.

4. Repeat steps 1 to 3 to make more flowers. You can experiment with size by making your circle larger or smaller.

5. If you want, you can paint the picture frame a colour of your choice. Let it dry.

6. Glue the paper flowers to the frame. Cover the entire frame or decorate a corner or two.

7. Put a photo of yourself and a loved one in the picture frame!

CINCO DE MAYO
# Papel picado banner

Cinco de Mayo, or the Fifth of May, commemorates the Battle of Puebla. In this 1862 battle, Mexico's army defeated French forces. Celebrate Mexico by making a banner inspired by *papel picado*, a Mexican folk art meaning "pecked paper".

## What you need

- pencil
- ruler
- cardboard
- scissors
- bottle top
- tissue paper
- felt pen
- craft knife (optional)
- painter's tape (optional)
- craft foam
- hot glue gun
- black paint and paintbrush
- plastic tray
- ribbon or string

## What you do

1. Cut out a 20 × 15-cm (8 × 6-in) cardboard rectangle. Use a bottle cap to draw a scalloped edge along one of the long sides.

2. Cut out the rectangle's scalloped edge. This will be a template for your papel picado.

3. Trace your template on a sheet of tissue paper using a felt pen.

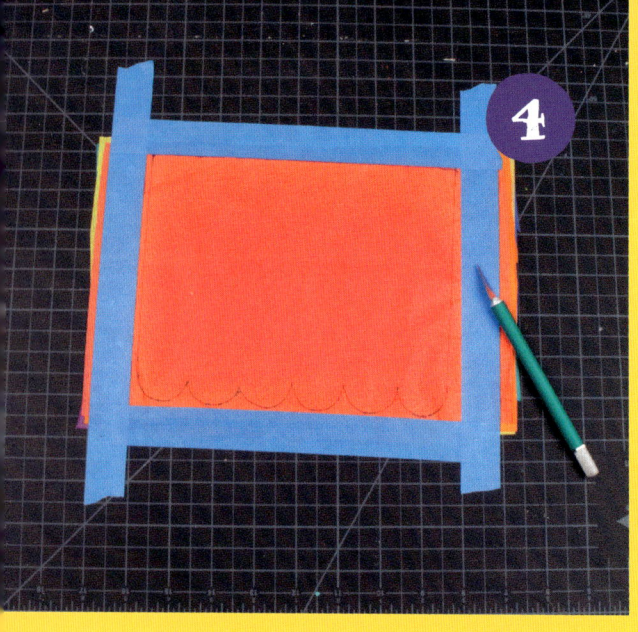

4. Place other sheets of tissue paper behind the first and cut them all out at once. This is easily done by taping the tissue paper layers to a work surface and carefully cutting them out with a craft knife. Ask an adult for help if you use a craft knife.

5. Cut triangles, circles and other small shapes out of craft foam. Glue the foam pieces to the paperboard template to create a papel picado stamp. If you want, you can look online for papel picado design inspiration.

6. Paint a thin layer of black paint on the bottom of a plastic tray. Dip your stamp in the paint. Use a small paintbrush to make sure the paint covers the craft foam pieces evenly.

7. Stamp your tissue paper flags with the papel picado design. You may have to re-dip your stamp for every one or two tissue paper flags.

8. Once your flags are dry, glue their non-scalloped long edges along a piece of ribbon or string. Then hang your banner!

# Fun fact

Many people confuse Cinco de Mayo with Mexico's Independence Day. But Mexico declared independence in 1810, more than 50 years before the Battle of Puebla.

# FIND OUT MORE

## BOOKS

*10-Minute Crafty Projects* (10-Minute Makers), Elsie Olson (Raintree, 2022)

*Celebrations Around the World* (Customs Around the World), Wil Mara (Raintree, 2021)

*Earth Day* (Traditions and Celebrations), Melissa Ferguson (Raintree, 2022)

## WEBSITES

**learnenglishkids.britishcouncil.org/category/topics/festivals-and-celebrations**
Find out about different world festivals and celebrations as well as some craft activities on this website.

**www.bbc.co.uk/cbbc/curations/bp-arts-and-crafts-collection**
CBBC has lots of craft ideas you can make.

## ABOUT THE AUTHOR

Megan Borgert-Spaniol is an author and editor of children's media. When she isn't writing or reading, she enjoys doing yoga, eating croissants and making homemade pizzas. Megan lives in Minneapolis, Minnesota, USA, with a tall, goofy man and a small, chatty cat.